Bond 11+

TEST PAPERS

Notes and Answers

Verbal Reasoning
Multiple Choice

Published by Nelson Thornes. Nelson Thornes is a Wolters Kluwer company, and is not associated in any way with NFER-Nelson.

Introduction

Background

Bond 11+ Test Papers have been produced to provide your child with realistic, formal practice for their actual examination(s) to select them for secondary school. We have tried to set out the papers in a style that is as close as possible to the real thing (which appears in different styles across the country), while preserving the unique style of *Bond Assessment Papers.*

However, since the difficulty of selection examinations varies across the country, and since grading depends to some extent on the overall standard of the candidates, the scores indicated by *Bond 11+ Test Papers* will not necessarily be an exact prediction of your child's final scores. The best way to ensure your child is as well prepared as possible is to give them as much practice as possible, and to allow them time to prepare as well as to practise. *Bond Assessment Papers* provide graded practice towards 11+ examinations, and can be used in tandem with *Bond 11+ Test Papers* to give your child an even better chance.

How to administer the tests

Try to provide a calm yet formal atmosphere in which your child can take the test. It is important that you re-create the real test as closely as possible, therefore there should be no distractions and an appropriate work-space for your child.

Read the front page of the test papers with your child, pointing out the importance of answering carefully but quickly, and moving on from questions they are stuck on before too much time has been wasted. Remind them that they can always go back at the end if they have time left.

Multiple Choice Tests ask children to mark their answers, in pencil, in the answer pages provided. These answer pages will, in the real test, be marked by computer. Your child must clearly, with a soft pencil, fill in the correct box relating to that question. Encourage your child to fill the answers in carefully, and to rub out any wrong answer, but NOT cross it out. You can ignore any of the boxes asking for pupil numbers, school numbers and so on – these are similar to the details required on the actual test papers and will help familiarise your child with the style of the actual examination paper.

Allow your child 50 minutes for each test. They can read the instructions before you 'start the clock'. When the time is up they should stop writing – you can always allow them to continue after the time to get more practice, or else leave the other questions blank for another day. Encourage them to think about whether they should try to speed up, or to work more carefully, depending on how they finish the paper.

Marking and Feedback

The answers that follow should be given 1 mark each unless otherwise indicated. Do not take marks away for wrong answers, but also do not award half marks. You can always talk to your child about answers that were 'nearly right', but you should not give them a mark. The process of preparing for an examination for selection should involve as much encouragement and assistance as possible.

Answers

Paper 1

1 t
2 k
3 m
4 e
5 t
6 y
7 a
8 e
9 quiet
10 desire
11 tranquil
12 brush
13 short
14 divide
15 ordinary
16 difficulty
17 % ^ ~ £
18 ! ^ ~ %
19 % £ £ #
20 SENSE
21 LINE
22 BIBLE
23 ? / > <
24 ? $ / < <
25 Monet was a painter.
26 Chairs can be made of wood.
27 DO DQ
28 XW NM
29 HJ NP
30 XI WG
31 IL JM
32 XU VS
33 jkl pqr
34 Ae Dh
35 BY CX
36 WILD
37 GRAB
38 WITH
39 HALT
40 DEER
41 STEP
42 OVEN
43 BIND (26)
44 tent
45 stop
46 hall
47 then
48 very
49 omen
50 fort
51 test
52 Suzy
53 Peter, Toby, Jon
54 Judy, Suzy
55 rainfall
56 anteater
57 playroom
58 inside
59 hindsight
60 foreleg
61 upright
62 byway
63 due sting
64 fight timer
65 bred rota
66 limb crack
67 play crumbs
68 lease spill
69 rain pleat
70 slit spin
71 hoses burns
72 crimson azure
73 impolite unpleasant
74 tiny huge
75 painter author
76 paw hoof
77 six eight
78 sleep play
79 sty cowshed
80 descend shrink

Paper 2

1 seat
2 vein
3 also
4 here
5 scar
6 form
7 soft
8 head
9 south
10 south
11 north east
12 1234
13 6421
14 YARD
15 ARTS
16 9348
17 5293
18 9345
19 5493
20 hurry
21 grass
22 nasty
23 honest
24 drawer
25 leader
26 fault
27 gravel
28 nested
29 s
30 p
31 r
32 p
33 s
34 q
35 t
36 q
37 spade
38 ring
39 bank
40 stable
41 fork
42 bolt
43 tie
44 hound
45 sow
46 t
47 k
48 l
49 t
50 ch
51 er
52 it
53 le
54 My house is made of cuboid bricks.
55 Goldfish breathe underwater.
56 FIST
57 COAT
58 RITE
59 TEAM
60 POUR
61 WINK
62 DAZE
63 SAID
64 right correct
65 dear expensive
66 tale fable
67 shut closed
68 weary tired
69 kind sort
70 evening night
71 hind buck
72 3 6
73 25 33
74 56 49
75 20 32
76 17 42
77 2 16
78 6 12
79 9 25
80 6 3

Paper 3

1 q m 5 v
2 2 m v 6
3 CART
4 RAIN
5 TASK
6 SEEK
7 7 j x 9
8 g 8 x 9 j
9 Peas are green vegetables.
10 Bees make sweet honey.
11 Caroline
12 Nick
13 Chris
14 meat
15 them
16 army
17 ours
18 veto
19 dent
20 best

21 reap
22 air water
23 brief amazing
24 cushion implement
25 slow dull
26 hard frightened
27 water tree
28 lumpy warm
29 lucid dirty
30 cut slice
31 sh
32 me
33 ar
34 ra
35 se
36 de
37 ee
38 in
39 VU PO
40 MN LO
41 AH AL
42 CO EQ
43 bh ci
44 WX CD
45 Bh Ek
46 XU TQ
47 CX GT
48 uneven
49 empty
50 active
51 wane
52 foe
53 weak
54 vast
55 found
56 photo
57 sauce
58 feast
59 start
60 drains
61 bleed
62 tests
63 overstay
64 ginger
65 PALM PALE
66 HARK HARE
67 WART WARS
68 BITE BILE
69 DAZE MAZE
70 FILE FILL
71 KING SING
72 FIST MIST
73 13
74 12
75 20
76 19
77 18
78 21
79 22
80 24

Paper 4

1 open closed
2 hide seek
3 tight loose
4 boiling freezing
5 begun ended
6 in out
7 light dark
8 fine thick
9 E
10 A
11 C
12 C
13 B
14 A
15 E
16 B
17 woodpecker
18 starlight
19 boardroom
20 breakfast
21 roundabout
22 throughout
23 whoever
24 outcome
25 arrow thank
26 rank patch
27 fight camel
28 cram breed
29 cane break
30 hose then
31 though frog
32 bat mouse
33 ray them
34 four
35 Class 1
36 Class 8
37 SALT SILT
38 HARE HIRE
39 QUIT SUIT
40 STEP SEEP
41 WINK WIND
42 WARS WART
43 POST PORT
44 FILE PILE
45 part
46 wave
47 dear
48 mine
49 stick
50 watch
51 groom
52 litter
53 march
54 20 23
55 50 35
56 20 40
57 33 18
58 13 71
59 6 48
60 30 6
61 8 32
62 16 10
63 scan
64 seat
65 this
66 fort
67 vest
68 chin
69 ship
70 hero
71 g p s l
72 t q p p o
73 KNIFE
74 SAUCER
75 TOMB
76 GROUND
77 c y p r f
78 j m u c q r
79 Leather shoes are waterproof.
80 Words can be written.

Published in 2003 by:
Nelson Thornes Ltd, Delta Place, 27 Bath Road
CHELTENHAM GL53 7TH, United Kingdom

05 06 07 / 10 9 8 7 6 5 4

A catalogue record for this book is available from the British Library

ISBN 0-7487-7327-4

Page make-up by IFA Design

Printed and bound in Croatia by Zrinski

Published by Nelson Thornes. Nelson Thornes is a Wolters Kluwer company, and is not associated in any way with NFER-Nelson.

Bond 11+

Verbal Reasoning

Multiple Choice Test 1

Read the following:

- Do not begin the test or open this booklet until told to do so.
- Work as quickly and as carefully as you can.
- Answers should be marked in the answer booklet provided, not in this test booklet.
- You may do rough working on a separate sheet of paper.
- If you make a mistake cross out the mistake and write the new answer clearly.
- Be careful to keep your place in the accompanying answer booklet.
- You will have 50 minutes to complete the test.

Published in 2003 by:
Nelson Thornes Ltd, Delta Place, 27 Bath Road
CHELTENHAM GL53 7TH, United Kingdom

05 06 07 / 10 9 8 7 6 5 4

A catalogue record for this book is available from the British Library

ISBN 0-7487-7327-4

Page make-up by IFA Design

Printed and bound in Croatia by Zrinski

Published by Nelson Thornes. Nelson Thornes is a Wolters Kluwer company, and is not associated in any way with NFER-Nelson.

Find the letter which will end the first word and start the second word.

Mark your answer in your answer booklet.

Example

d r o w (**n**) o u g h t

1 p a r (....) r a p

2 t a l (....) n i t

3 f a r (....) a i n

4 k i t (....) d i t

5 s a l (....) o o l

6 f o x (....) o l k

7 s a g (....) l s o

8 p i n (....) v e n

CONTINUE

Choose the one word in the brackets closest in meaning to the word above the brackets.

Mark your answer in your answer booklet.

Example

unhappy
(unkind, death, laughter, sad, friendly)

9 still
(alone, always, drink, quiet, quite)

10 long
(short, mile, high, low, desire)

11 calm
(balm, tranquil, cream, storm, tide)

12 broom
(bride, car, brush, vanish, stick)

13 brief
(case, shorts, minimum, sudden, short)

14 part
(divide, fracture, whole, chorus, play)

15 common
(grass, garden, weed, unusual, ordinary)

16 problem
(sum, hard, solution, difficulty, impossible)

CONTINUE

In a code the word **HOMEWORK** is written as *** ^ % £ ! ^ ~ #**.

Work out the codes for each of these words.

Mark your answer in your answer booklet.

17 MORE

18 WORM

19 MEEK

< £ > < / ? $ £ is the code word for **SENSIBLE** .

Decode these symbols.

Mark your answer in your answer booklet.

20 < £ > < £

21 $ / > £

22 ? / ? $ £

Encode these words.

Mark your answer in your answer booklet.

23 BINS

24 BLISS

CONTINUE

From the four choices, choose the one statement which must be true.

Mark your answer in your answer booklet.

Example

Lions are animals. Animals are not stone.

Lions are cruel.
Lions are flesh.
Lions are not stone.
Lions are animals because they hunt.

25 *Monet painted poppies.*

Pictures consist of paint.
Monet liked poppies.
Monet was a painter.
Poppies need red paint.

26 *Chairs are furniture. Furniture can be made of wood.*

Chairs can be made of wood.
Trees supply wood.
Wood is used for all furniture.
Trees are furniture because they are wood.

CONTINUE TO THE NEXT PAGE

Find the two missing groups of letters in the following sequences.

Mark your answer in your answer booklet.

A B C D E F G H I J K L M
N O P Q R S T U V W X Y Z

Example

	CQ	DQ	EP	FP	**GO**	**HO**
27	BG	BI	CK	CM	....	....
28	....	VU	TS	RQ	PO	....
29	BD	EG	....	KM	....	QS
30	XJ	....	WH	....	VF	VE
31	....	....	KN	LO	MP	NQ
32	ZW	YV	....	WT	....	UR
33	ABC	def	GHI	....	MNO	....
34	....	Bf	Cg	....	Ei	Fj
35	AZ	....	....	DW	EV	FU

CONTINUE

Change the first word into the last word by changing one letter at a time and making a new, different word in the middle.

Mark your answer in your answer booklet.

Example

	CASE	....	LASH
	CASE	**CASH**	LASH
36	WILL	....	WIND
37	CRAB	....	GRUB
38	PITH	....	WISH
39	HALL	....	SALT
40	JEER	....	DEAR
41	STOP	....	STEM
42	OXEN	....	EVEN
43	KIND	....	BAND

CONTINUE

Find the four-letter word hidden at the end of one word and the beginning of the next word in these sentences. The order of the letters may not be changed.

Mark your answer in your answer booklet.

Example

We had bat**s and** balls.

44 Listen to her advice carefully.

45 My dentist opened the surgery door.

46 I wish all my class could come to the party.

47 Come to the back door of the new building.

48 The squid stretched a tentacle over yellow weed.

49 Take your litter home, never drop it.

50 The weather forecast for this evening is appalling.

51 The kite string was caught in the tree.

CONTINUE

Class 1 were doing a survey of favourite drinks. Here are the results of one group:

Paul and Judy like tea, squash and cola.
Peter, Beth and Toby like lemonade.
Suzy and Jon like squash, lemonade and juice.
Emily, Sue and Gary like cola and milk.
All the girls also like soda.

Answer the following questions.

Mark your answer in your answer booklet.

52 Which people like soda and juice?

53 Which people like lemonade but not soda?

54 Which people like the most drinks?

CONTINUE TO THE NEXT PAGE

Choose two words, one from each group, that go together to form a new word. The word in the first group always comes first.

Mark your answer in your answer booklet.

Example

	(hand, <u>green</u>, for)	(light, <u>house</u>, sure)
55	(sun, cloud, rain)	(shone, fall, pour)
56	(moth, ant, frog)	(hop, eater, tick)
57	(act, play, sausage)	(role, cast, room)
58	(at, by, in)	(side, wide, last)
59	(hind, right, rain)	(sight, deer, fell)
60	(for, four, fore)	(gear, place, leg)
61	(up, under, stand)	(left, right, sit)
62	(to, by, in)	(age, way, held)

CONTINUE

Move one letter from the first word to the second word to make two new words.

Mark your answer in your answer booklet.

Example

	hunt	sip	<u>hut</u>	<u>snip</u>
63	duet	sing		
64	fright	time		
65	bread	rot		
66	climb	rack		
67	splay	crumb		
68	please	sill		
69	train	plea		
70	split	sin		
71	horses	buns		

CONTINUE

Complete the following sentences in the best way by choosing one word from each set of brackets.

Mark your answer in your answer booklet.

Example

Tall is to (tree, short, colour)
as narrow is to (thin, white, wide).

72 Red is to (colour, crimson, danger)
as blue is to (paint, cloud, azure).

73 Polite is to (impolite, rude, manners)
as pleasant is to (unpleasant, nasty, sunny).

74 Minute is to (hour, tiny, second)
as vast is to (clock, time, huge).

75 Picture is to (paint, painter, brush)
as book is to (artist, page, author).

76 Dog is to (collar, paw, bark)
as horse is to (saddle, hoof, stable).

77 Beetle is to (six, insect, ladybird)
as spider is to (web, eight, spin).

78 Bed is to (bedroom, sheet, sleep)
as game is to (football, chess, play).

79 Pig is to (sty, pork, mud)
as cow is to (milk, moo, cowshed).

80 Climb is to (mountain, ascend, descend)
as grow is to (compost, age, shrink).

Bond 11+

Verbal Reasoning

Multiple Choice Test 2

Read the following:

- Do not begin the test or open this booklet until told to do so.
- Work as quickly and as carefully as you can.
- Answers should be marked in the answer booklet provided, not in this test booklet.
- You may do rough working on a separate sheet of paper.
- If you make a mistake cross out the mistake and write the new answer clearly.
- Be careful to keep your place in the accompanying answer booklet.
- You will have 50 minutes to complete the test.

Published in 2003 by:
Nelson Thornes Ltd, Delta Place, 27 Bath Road
CHELTENHAM GL53 7TH, United Kingdom

05 06 07 / 10 9 8 7 6 5 4

A catalogue record for this book is available from the British Library

ISBN 0-7487-7327-4

Page make-up by IFA Design

Printed and bound in Croatia by Zrinski

Published by Nelson Thornes. Nelson Thornes is a Wolters Kluwer company, and is not associated in any way with NFER-Nelson.

Find the four-letter word hidden at the end of one word and the beginning of the next word in these sentences. The order of the letters may not be changed.

Mark your answer in your answer booklet.

Example

We had bat**s and** balls.

1 Pigs eat different sorts of scraps.

2 Please do not leave in such a rush.

3 Jack's solo was in the final song.

4 It would be better to go another evening.

5 Sarah's car would not start this morning.

6 Climbing a mountain is a challenge for most people.

7 Biscuits often contain high levels of sugar.

8 Amy immediately posted her cards as she addressed them.

CONTINUE

David's house is west of the Post Office and southwest of the farm.

The farm is due east of the school.
The school is north west of the Post Office.
These four places form the points of a square.

Answer the following questions.

Mark your answer in your answer booklet.

9 Where is the Post Office in relation to the farm?

10 Where is David's house in relation to the school?

11 Where is the farm in relation to David's house?

CONTINUE

In a code the word **YESTERDAY** is written as **7 4 9 3 4 1 6 2 7**.

Work out the codes for each of these words.

Mark your answer in your answer booklet.

12 RATE

13 DEAR

Decode these numbers.

Mark your answer in your answer booklet.

14 7 2 1 6

15 2 1 3 9

CONTINUE

Here are four number codes. Match them to the correct words.

Mark your answer in your answer booklet.

9 3 4 5 **5 4 9 3** **9 3 4 8** **5 2 9 3**

16 STEM

17 PAST

18 STEP

19 PEST

CONTINUE TO THE NEXT PAGE

Select the one word in each group which **cannot** be made from the letters of the word in capital letters.

Mark your answer in your answer booklet.

Example

STATIONERY

stone	tyres	ration	<u>nation</u>	noisy

20 THURSDAY

shard	dusty	thuds	rusty	hurry

21 PLASTERING

staring	string	laser	grass	strain

22 BANNISTER

nasty	stern	banter	rinse	tribe

23 SILHOUETTE

house	honest	teeth	heels	those

24 ANSWERED

swear	drawer	snared	swede	waned

25 DREADFUL

fared	leader	flared	deaf	ladder

26 CAULIFLOWER

flower	fault	crow	frolic	crawl

27 FLAVOURING

fling	valour	gravel	grain	flour

28 STRAINED

drain	darts	dines	snare	nested

CONTINUE

If **p = 6**, **q = 4**, **r = 2**, **s = 12** and **t = 8**, give the answers to these sums as letters.

Mark your answer in your answer booklet.

29 $p \times r =$

30 s divided by r =

31 $(p \times q)$ divided by s =

32 $(t + q)$ divided by r =

33 $p + q + r =$

34 $s - p - r =$

35 $(s \times r) - (t \times r) =$

36 $r \times t$ divided by q =

CONTINUE

Choose the one word in the brackets which will go equally well with both the pairs of words or phrases outside the brackets.

Mark your answer in your answer booklet.

Example

rush, attack   cost, fee
(price, hasten, strike, charge, money)

37 club, diamond   hoe, rake
(weapon, spade, jewel, garden, heart)

38 bracelet, necklace   telephone, bell
(wedding, ring, line, valuable, rich)

39 mound, river edge   cash, credit card
(pile, fence, cheque, ditch, bank)

40 firm, safe   horse, shelter
(stable, ride, house, reliable, sound)

41 knife, spoon   divide, part
(fraction, fork, cutlery, cut, food)

42 run, flee   lock, fasten
(fortify, key, bolt, escape, hide)

43 shirt, collar   attach, bind
(suit, bond, chest, neck, tie)

44 chase, follow   wolf, fox
(pursue, run, hound, jackal, hunt)

45 piglet, boar   plant, drill
(pig, seed, farm, sow, hole)

CONTINUE

Find the letter which will end the first word and start the second word.

Mark your answer in your answer booklet.

Example

d r o w (**n**) o u g h t

46 s a l (....) o a d

47 p i n (....) i n d

48 t e l (....) o v e

49 s o f (....) r i m

CONTINUE TO THE NEXT PAGE

Find the two letters which will end the first word and start the second word.

Mark your answer in your answer booklet.

Example

r e a (**c h**) a i r

50 b e n (....) a i n

51 p r a y (....) m i n e

52 b i s c u (....) e m

53 s t a b (....) a d e n

CONTINUE

From the four choices, choose the one statement which must be true.

Mark your answer in your answer booklet.

Example

Lions are animals. Animals are not stone.

Lions are cruel.
Lions are flesh.
<u>Lions are not stone.</u>
Lions are animals because they hunt.

54 *My house is made of brick. Bricks are cuboid.*

My next door neighbour's house is made of brick.
My house is a cuboid.
My house is made of cuboid bricks.
All houses are brick.

55 *Fish breathe underwater. Goldfish live in fresh water.*

Goldfish make good pets.
The seas are full of fish.
Goldfish breathe underwater.
Cod and mackerel live in the sea.

CONTINUE

Change the first word into the last word by changing one letter at a time and making a new, different word in the middle.

Mark your answer in your answer booklet.

Example

	CASE	....	LASH
	CASE	CASH	LASH
56	FISH	....	MIST
57	COST	....	COAL
58	SITE	....	ROTE
59	SEAM	....	TEAK
60	FOUR	....	POOR
61	WIND	....	SINK
62	DOZE	....	MAZE
63	SAIL	....	SAND

CONTINUE

Select the two words, one from each group, which are closest in meaning.

Mark your answer in your answer booklet.

Example

	(race, shop, start)	(finish, begin, end)
64	(right, hand, finger)	(left, foot, correct)
65	(beloved, cheap, dear)	(expensive, love, antelope)
66	(tale, feeble, rat)	(small, mouse, fable)
67	(open, shut, window)	(closed, ajar, pane)
68	(weary, fresh, asleep)	(stale, tired, awake)
69	(kind, thoughtful, part)	(unkind, whole, sort)
70	(black, day, evening)	(white, night, light)
71	(pail, hind, fore)	(dark, three, buck)

CONTINUE TO THE NEXT PAGE

Find the two missing numbers in the following sequences.

Mark your answer in your answer booklet.

Example

	2	4	6	8	**10**	**12**
72	....	....	9	12	15	18
73	17	21	....	29	....	37
74	63	....	....	42	35	28
75	16	36	18	34	....	....
76	....	22	27	32	37	....
77	....	4	8	....	32	64
78	3	4	....	8	9	....
79	15	....	20	18	....	27
80	96	48	24	12	....	....

Bond 11+

Verbal Reasoning

Multiple Choice Test 3

Read the following:

- Do not begin the test or open this booklet until told to do so.
- Work as quickly and as carefully as you can.
- Answers should be marked in the answer booklet provided, not in this test booklet.
- You may do rough working on a separate sheet of paper.
- If you make a mistake cross out the mistake and write the new answer clearly.
- Be careful to keep your place in the accompanying answer booklet.
- You will have 50 minutes to complete the test.

Published in 2003 by:
Nelson Thornes Ltd, Delta Place, 27 Bath Road
CHELTENHAM GL53 7TH, United Kingdom

05 06 07 / 10 9 8 7 6 5 4

A catalogue record for this book is available from the British Library

ISBN 0-7487-7327-4

Page make-up by IFA Design

Printed and bound in Croatia by Zrinski

Published by Nelson Thornes. Nelson Thornes is a Wolters Kluwer company, and is not associated in any way with NFER-Nelson.

In a code the word **FRACTION** is written as **2 5 z q 6 w m v**.

Work out the codes for each of these words.

Mark your answer in your answer booklet.

1 CORN

2 FONT

Decode these letters and numbers.

Mark your answer in your answer booklet.

3 q z 5 6

4 5 z w v

In a code, the word **BASKET** is written as **7 x g 8 j 9**.

Decode these letters and numbers.

Mark your answer in your answer booklet.

5 9 x g 8

6 g j j 8

Encode these words.

Mark your answer in your answer booklet.

7 BEAT

8 SKATE

CONTINUE

From the four choices, choose the one statement which must be true.

Mark your answer in your answer booklet.

Example

Lions are animals. Animals are not stone.

Lions are cruel.
Lions are flesh.
<u>Lions are not stone.</u>
Lions are animals because they hunt.

9 *Peas are green. Peas are vegetables.*

Vegetables are green.
All green things are vegetables.
Vegetables are peas.
Peas are green vegetables.

10 *Bees make honey. Honey tastes sweet.*

Bees are sweet.
Everyone likes honey.
Bees make sweet honey.
Bees can sting.

CONTINUE

Claire, Nick and Chris wore blue shorts.
Nick, Caroline and Sue wore white shirts.
Sue, David and Caroline wore blue jeans.
David, Caroline and Claire wore red jerseys.
Chris, David and Claire wore blue shirts.
Sue, Nick and Chris wore blue jerseys.

Answer the following questions.

Mark your answer in your answer booklet.

11 Who wore a white shirt, blue jeans and a red jersey?

12 Who wore a white shirt with blue shorts?

13 Who wore entirely blue?

CONTINUE

Find the four-letter word hidden at the end of one word and the beginning of the next word in these sentences. The order of the letters may not be changed.

Mark your answer in your answer booklet.

Example

We had bat**s and** balls.

14 William, please come at once.

15 The sunset bathed the mountain in golden light.

16 The river is flooding near my house.

17 The pavement on our street is very uneven.

18 We have too much homework tonight.

19 Sailors told of mermaids combing their golden tresses.

20 The floorboards are known to be structurally unsound.

21 Their apples were apparently rotten.

CONTINUE TO THE NEXT PAGE

Complete the following sentences in the best way by choosing one word from each set of brackets.

Mark your answer in your answer booklet.

Example

Tall is to (tree, short, colour)
as narrow is to (thin, white, wide).

22 Aeroplane is to (air, fly, airport)
as submarine is to (water, periscope, metal).

23 Short is to (shirt, long, brief)
as incredible is to (believable, edible, amazing).

24 Pillow is to (cushion, bed, feathers)
as pitchfork is to (implement, spoon, hay).

25 Fast is to (slow, quick, tight)
as bright is to (sun, metal, dull).

26 Arduous is to (hard, easy, ardent)
as scared is to (sacred, spooky, frightened).

27 River is to (water, bank, boat)
as forest is to (shady, tree, branch).

28 Flat is to (bungalow, lumpy, house)
as cool is to (warm, cold, icy).

29 Clear is to (clean, see, lucid)
as unclean is to (clean, dirty, wash).

30 Saw is to (eye, vision, cut)
as knife is to (slice, spoon, utensil).

CONTINUE

Find the two letters which will end the first word and start the second word.

Mark your answer in your answer booklet.

Example

rea(**ch**)air

31 cra(....)utter

32 sha(....)et

33 cle(....)ea

34 came(....)nge

35 crea(....)ven

36 spa(....)cide

37 toff(....)rie

38 curta(....)side

CONTINUE

Find the two missing groups of letters in the following sequences.

Mark your answer in your answer booklet.

A B C D E F G H I J K L M
N O P Q R S T U V W X Y Z

Example

	CQ	DQ	EP	FP	**GO**	**HO**
39	ZY	XW	....	TS	RQ	....
40	....	....	KP	JQ	IR	HS
41	AB	AD	AF	....	AJ	....
42	AM	BN	....	DP	....	FR
43	ae	af	bg	....	....	cj
44	....	ST	OP	KL	GH	....
45	Ag	....	Ci	Dj	....	Fl
46	....	VS	....	RO	PM	NK
47	AZ	....	EV	....	IR	KP

CONTINUE

Choose one word from those in the brackets which is opposite in meaning to the word outside the brackets.

Mark your answer in your answer booklet.

Example

wide
(broad, vague, long, <u>narrow</u>, motorway)

48 level
(downhill, crossing, even, uneven, upright)

49 full
(empty, drink, eaten, laden, replete)

50 still
(silent, motionless, active, photo, even)

51 wax
(candle, wick, wane, ruby, dry)

52 friend
(neighbour, opponent, mate, colleague, foe)

53 strong
(flavour, tasteless, weak, robust, tasty)

54 minute
(hour, second, tiny, vast, invisible)

55 lost
(find, found, finding, finds, founded)

CONTINUE TO THE NEXT PAGE

Select the one word in each group which cannot be made from the letters of the word in capital letters.

Mark your answer in your answer booklet.

Example

STATIONERY

stone	tyres	ration	<u>nation</u>	noisy

56 TELEPHONES

shone	pole	photo	honest	spent

57 STATUES

astute	suet	uses	sauce	states

58 PETRIFIES

fires	feast	spite	trees	rites

59 CHRISTMAS

smith	chasm	match	charm	start

60 RADISHES

shade	rashes	dress	shares	drains

61 BREAKABLE

bleak	area	leer	bleed	rabble

62 POTATOES

state	tests	soap	taste	post

63 CONTROVERSY

strove	sorry	overstay	very	store

64 BELONGINGS

singe	longing	ginger	lobes	gongs

CONTINUE

Change the first word into the last word by changing one letter at a time and making two new, different words in the middle.

Mark your answer in your answer booklet.

Example

	PEAS	....	....	RENT
	PEAS	**PENS**	**PENT**	RENT
65	CALM	....	....	POLE
66	LARK	....	....	HAZE
67	WAIT	....	....	JARS
68	SITE	....	....	BILL
69	DOZE	....	....	MADE
70	FIRE	....	....	FALL
71	KIND	....	....	SUNG
72	FISH	....	....	MUST

CONTINUE

If **s = 3**, **e = 2**, **r = 5**, **a = 1**, **t = 6** and **d = 4**, find the value of the following words by adding the letters together.

Mark your answer in your answer booklet.

73 deer

74 read

75 treat

76 darts

77 tread

78 stared

79 rested

80 dresser

Bond 11+

Verbal Reasoning

Multiple Choice Test 4

Read the following:

- Do not begin the test or open this booklet until told to do so.
- Work as quickly and as carefully as you can.
- Answers should be marked in the answer booklet provided, not in this test booklet.
- You may do rough working on a separate sheet of paper.
- If you make a mistake cross out the mistake and write the new answer clearly.
- Be careful to keep your place in the accompanying answer booklet.
- You will have 50 minutes to complete the test.

Published in 2003 by:
Nelson Thornes Ltd, Delta Place, 27 Bath Road
CHELTENHAM GL53 7TH, United Kingdom

05 06 07 / 10 9 8 7 6 5 4

A catalogue record for this book is available from the British Library

ISBN 0-7487-7327-4

Page make-up by IFA Design

Printed and bound in Croatia by Zrinski

Published by Nelson Thornes. Nelson Thornes is a Wolters Kluwer company, and is not associated in any way with NFER-Nelson.

Find the two words, one from each group, which are opposite in meaning.

Mark your answer in your answer booklet.

Example

	(dawn, early, awake)	(late, stop, sunrise)
1	(open, shut, near)	(closed, ajar, unfenced)
2	(skin, hide, bear)	(burden, look, seek)
3	(tight, noose, slack)	(fast, loose, hang)
4	(boiling, warm, hot)	(cooler, sweat, freezing)
5	(begun, begin, finished)	(ended, ending, ends)
6	(under, on, in)	(out, below, through)
7	(moon, light, night)	(star, sky, dark)
8	(fine, fancy, ill)	(dress, dirty, thick)

CONTINUE

If **A = 2**, **B = 4**, **C = 5**, **D = 10** and **E = 8**, give the answers to these sums as letters.

Mark your answer in your answer booklet.

9 $A + D - B =$

10 D divided by C =

11 $C \times D$ divided by $(A + E) =$

12 $D \times A$ divided by B =

13 $C \times E$ divided by D =

14 $(E + B) - D =$

15 B squared divided by A =

16 $(B \times D) - E$ divided by E =

CONTINUE

Choose two words, one from each group, that go together to form a new word. The word in the first group always comes first.

Mark your answer in your answer booklet.

Example

	(hand, <u>green</u>, for)	(light, <u>house</u>, sure)
17	(tree, wood, branch)	(picker, pecker, packer)
18	(star, house, home)	(trek, super, light)
19	(board, coffee, runner)	(cup, room, been)
20	(flow, break, time)	(slow, fast, minute)
21	(short, fall, round)	(about, circle, climb)
22	(through, in, though)	(sign, full, out)
23	(some, who, odd)	(even, ever, out)
24	(through, by, out)	(all, hold, come)

CONTINUE

Move one letter from the first word to the second word to make two new words.

Mark your answer in your answer booklet.

Example

	hunt	sip	<u>hut</u>	<u>snip</u>
25	harrow	tank		
26	crank	path		
27	flight	came		
28	cream	bred		
29	crane	beak		
30	those	hen		
31	through	fog		
32	boat	muse		
33	tray	hem		

CONTINUE TO THE NEXT PAGE

On Thursdays, Classes 7, 4, 6 and 8 have Music.
Classes 4, 3, 6 and 7 have French.
Classes 1, 6 and 3 have Geography.
All the classes except 6 have Maths.
Classes 2, 5, 6 and 8 have P.E.

Answer the following questions.

Mark your answer in your answer booklet.

34 How many of these lessons does Class 6 have?

35 Which class does Geography but not French?

36 Which class does P.E., Maths and Music?

CONTINUE

Change the first word into the last word by changing one letter at a time and making two new, different words in the middle.

Mark your answer in your answer booklet.

Example

	PEAS	....	....	RENT
	PEAS	**PENS**	**PENT**	RENT
37	SALE	....	....	WILT
38	HARP	....	....	HIDE
39	QUIZ	....	....	SUET
40	STOP	....	....	WEEP
41	PINK	....	....	WILD
42	JARS	....	....	WANT
43	MOST	....	....	PORK
44	FILM	....	....	PALE

CONTINUE

Choose the one word in the brackets which will go equally well with both the pairs of words outside the brackets.

Mark your answer in your answer booklet.

Example

rush, attack — cost, fee
(price, hasten, strike, <u>charge</u>, money)

45 role, play — fraction, division
(scene, part, leave, school, sum)

46 sea, shore — greet, salute
(shell, tide, recognise, see, wave)

47 love, darling — expensive, costly
(price, dear, sweet, cheap, kind)

48 hers, ours — coal, gold
(possess, ore, mine, belong, pit)

49 glue, adhere — twig, wood
(stick, leaf, tree, tack, mend)

50 clock, time — observe, spy
(second, examine, tell, follow, watch)

51 jockey, horse — bride, wedding
(bridle, groom, jump, hat, bell)

52 rubbish, waste — carriage, chair
(dustbin, lorry, tip, litter, table)

53 season, month — soldier, parade
(may, gun, spring, boot, march)

CONTINUE

Find the two missing numbers in the following sequences.

Mark your answer in your answer booklet.

Example

	2	4	6	8	**10**	**12**
54	17	....	....	26	29	32
55	....	45	40	....	30	25
56	5	10	....	....	80	160
57	11	14	22	16	....	....
58	91	....	81	17	....	21
59	....	12	24	....	96	192
60	35	4	....	5	25	....
61	....	....	16	16	32	8
62	50	40	31	23	....	....

CONTINUE TO THE NEXT PAGE

Find the four-letter word hidden at the end of one word and the beginning of the next word in these sentences. The order of the letters may not be changed.

Mark your answer in your answer booklet.

Example

We had bat**s and** balls.

63 Dates can be found on palm trees.

64 Please attach your pencils to your clipboards.

65 The small boy lost his mother in the crowd.

66 Tom's spectacular save ensured victory for the home side.

67 Waves tumbled and crashed on the shingle.

68 The cheetah can reach incredible speeds over short distances.

69 An old man fell on the ice and broke his hip.

70 Amy wanted to sit in the row in front of Neil.

CONTINUE

A B C D E F G H I J K L M
N O P Q R S T U V W X Y Z

In a code the word **PLATE** is written as **q m b u f**.

Work out the codes for each of these words.

Mark your answer in your answer booklet.

71 FORK

72 SPOON

Decode these letters.

Mark your answer in your answer booklet.

73 l o j g f

74 t b v d f s

In code, the word **BOTTOM** is written as **z m r r m k**.

Decode these letters.

Mark your answer in your answer booklet.

75 r m k z

76 e p m s l b

Encode these words.

Mark your answer in your answer booklet.

77 EARTH

78 LOWEST

CONTINUE

From the four choices, choose the one statement which must be true.

Mark your answer in your answer booklet.

Example

Lions are animals. Animals are not stone.

Lions are cruel.
Lions are flesh.
Lions are not stone.
Lions are animals because they hunt.

79 *Some shoes are made from leather. Leather is waterproof.*

Shoes are worn with socks.
All shoes are made from leather.
Leather shoes are waterproof.
Leather is the best material for shoes.

80 *Words are made of letters. Letters can be written.*

All words are written.
Sentences are made of words.
Letters are always written with a pen.
Words can be written.

Bond 11+

TEST PAPERS

Answer sheets for Multiple Choice Tests

All of the answer sheets for Bond 11+ Test Papers Multiple-Choice versions are included in this booklet. Please ensure you are using the correct answer sheet for the test you are taking. The tests covered in this booklet are Maths 1–4, Non-verbal Reasoning 1–4 and Verbal Reasoning 1–4.

Published in 2003 by:
Nelson Thornes Ltd
Delta Place
27 Bath Road
CHELTENHAM
GL53 7TH
United Kingdom

05 06 07 / 10 9 8 7 6 5 4

A catalogue record for this book is available from the British Library

ISBN 0-7487-7327-4

Page make-up by IFA Design Ltd, Plymouth, Devon

Printed and bound in Croatia by Zrinski

Published by Nelson Thornes. Nelson Thornes is a Wolters Kluwer company, and is not associated in any way with NFER-Nelson.

Bond 11+ Maths Test 1

Name

1 D E F G H	2 A B C D E	3 A B C D E	4 A B C D E	5 A B C D E	6 P Q R S T	7 A B C D E
8 A B C D E	9 A B C D E	10 A B C D E	11 A B C D E	12 A B C D E	13 A B C D E	14 A B C D E
15 A B C D E	16 A B C D E	17 A B C D E	18 A B C D E	19 A B C D E	20 A B C D E	21 A B C D E
22 A B C D E	23 A B C D E	24 A B C D E	25 A B C D E	26 A B C D E	27 A B C D E	28 A B C D E
29 A B C D E	30 A B C D E	31 A B C D E	32 A B C D E	33 A B C D E	34 A B C D E	35 A B C D E
36 A B C D E	37 A B C D E	38 A B C D E	39 A B C D E	40 A B C D E	41 A B C D E	42 A B C D E

43 A B C D E	44 A B C D E	45 A B C D E	46 A B C D E	47 A B C D E	48 A B C D E	49 A B C D E	50 A B C D E

Bond 11+ Maths Test 2

Name

1	2	3	4	5	6	7
A B C D E	A B C D E	A B C D E	A B C D E	A B C D E	A B C D E	A B C D E

8	9	10	11	12	13	14
A B C D E	A B C D E	A B C D E	A B C D E	A B C D E	A B C D E	A B C D E

15	16	17	18	19	20	21
A B C D E	A B C D E	A B C D E	A B C D E	A B C D E	A B C D E	A B C D E

22	23	24	25	26	27	28
A B C D E	A B C D E	A B C D E	A B C D E	A B C D E	A B C D E	A B C D E

29	30	31	32	33	34	35
A B C D E	A B C D E	A B C D E	A B C D E	A B C D E	A B C D E	A B C D E

36	37	38	39	40	41	42
A B C D E	A B C D E	A B C D E	A B C D E	A B C D E	A B C D E	A B C D E

43	44	45	46	47	48	49	50
A B C D E	A B C D E	A B C D E	A B C D E	A B C D E	A B C D E	A B C D E	A B C D E

Bond 11+ Maths Test 3

Name

1	A B C D E
2	A B C D E
3	A B C D E
4	A B C D E
5	A B C D E
6	A B C D E
7	A B C D E
8	A B C D E
9	A B C D E
10	A B C D E
11	A B C D E
12	A B C D E
13	A B C D E
14	A B C D E
15	A B C D E
16	A B C D E
17	A B C D E
18	A B C D E
19	COX NON DAD MUM HIT
20	A B C D E
21	A B C D E
22	A B C D E
23	A B C D E
24	A B C D E
25	A B C D E
26	A B C D E
27	A B C D E
28	A B C D E
29	A B C D E
30	A B C D E
31	A B C D E
32	A B C D E
33	A B C D E
34	A B C D E
35	A B C D E
36	A B C D E
37	A B C D E
38	A B C D E
39	A B C D E
40	A B C D E
41	A B C D E
42	A B C D E
43	A B C D E
44	R S T U V
45	A B C D E
46	A B C D E
47	A B C D E
48	A B C D E
49	A B C D E
50	A B C D E

 Published by Nelson Thornes. Nelson Thornes is a Wolters Kluwer company, and is not associated in any way with NFER-Nelson.

Bond 11+ Maths Test 4

Name

1 A B C D E

2 A B C D E

3 A B C D E

4 A B C D E

5 A B C D E

6 A B C D E

7 A B C D E

8 A B C D E

9 A B C D E

10 A B C D E

11 A B C D E

12 A B C D E

13 A B C D E

14 A B C D E

15 A B C D E

16 A B C D E

17 A B C D E

18 A B C D E

19 A B C D E

20 A B C D E

21 A B C D E

22 A B C D E

23 A B C D E

24 A B C D E

25 A B C D E

26 A B C D E

27 A B C D E

28 NOZE NOS HOSE ICON TON

29 A B C D E

30 A B C D E

31 A B C D E

32 A B C D E

33 A B C D E

34 A B C D E

35 A B C D E

36 A B C D E

37 A B C D E

38 A B C D E

39 A B C D E

40 A B C D E

41 A B C D E

42 A B C D E

43 A B C D E

44 A B C D E

45 A B C D E

46 A B C D E

47 A B C D E

48 A B C D E

49 A B C D E

50 A B C D E

Bond 11+ Non-verbal Reasoning Test 1

Name

Section 1

Practice 1	a b c d e
Practice 2	a b c d e
1	a b c d e
2	a b c d e
3	a b c d e
4	a b c d e
5	a b c d e
6	a b c d e
7	a b c d e
8	a b c d e
9	a b c d e
10	a b c d e
11	a b c d e
12	a b c d e

Section 2

Practice 1	a b c d e
Practice 2	a b c d e
1	a b c d e
2	a b c d e
3	a b c d e
4	a b c d e
5	a b c d e
6	a b c d e
7	a b c d e
8	a b c d e
9	a b c d e
10	a b c d e
11	a b c d e
12	a b c d e

Section 3

Practice 1	a b c d e
Practice 2	a b c d e
1	a b c d e
2	a b c d e
3	a b c d e
4	a b c d e
5	a b c d e
6	a b c d e
7	a b c d e
8	a b c d e
9	a b c d e
10	a b c d e
11	a b c d e
12	a b c d e

Section 4

Practice 1	a b c d e
Practice 2	a b c d e
1	a b c d e
2	a b c d e
3	a b c d e
4	a b c d e
5	a b c d e
6	a b c d e
7	a b c d e
8	a b c d e
9	a b c d e
10	a b c d e
11	a b c d e
12	a b c d e

Section 5

Practice 1	a b c d e
Practice 2	a b c d e
1	a b c d e
2	a b c d e
3	a b c d e
4	a b c d e
5	a b c d e
6	a b c d e
7	a b c d e
8	a b c d e
9	a b c d e
10	a b c d e
11	a b c d e
12	a b c d e

Bond 11+ Non-verbal Reasoning Test 2

Name

Section 1

Practice 1	Practice 2	1	2	3	4	5	6	7	8	9	10	11	12
a	a	a	a	a	a	a	a	a	a	a	a	a	a
b	b	b	b	b	b	b	b	b	b	b	b	b	b
c	c	c	c	c	c	c	c	c	c	c	c	c	c
d	d	d	d	d	d	d	d	d	d	d	d	d	d
e	e	e	e	e	e	e	e	e	e	e	e	e	e

Section 2

Practice 1	Practice 2	1	2	3	4	5	6	7	8	9	10	11	12
a	a	a	a	a	a	a	a	a	a	a	a	a	a
b	b	b	b	b	b	b	b	b	b	b	b	b	b
c	c	c	c	c	c	c	c	c	c	c	c	c	c
d	d	d	d	d	d	d	d	d	d	d	d	d	d
e	e	e	e	e	e	e	e	e	e	e	e	e	e

Section 3

Practice 1	Practice 2	1	2	3	4	5	6	7	8	9	10	11	12
a	a	a	a	a	a	a	a	a	a	a	a	a	a
b	b	b	b	b	b	b	b	b	b	b	b	b	b
c	c	c	c	c	c	c	c	c	c	c	c	c	c
d	d	d	d	d	d	d	d	d	d	d	d	d	d
e	e	e	e	e	e	e	e	e	e	e	e	e	e

Section 4

Practice 1	Practice 2	1	2	3	4	5	6	7	8	9	10	11	12
a	a	a	a	a	a	a	a	a	a	a	a	a	a
b	b	b	b	b	b	b	b	b	b	b	b	b	b
c	c	c	c	c	c	c	c	c	c	c	c	c	c
d	d	d	d	d	d	d	d	d	d	d	d	d	d
e	e	e	e	e	e	e	e	e	e	e	e	e	e

Section 5

Practice 1	Practice 2	1	2	3	4	5	6	7	8	9	10	11	12
a	a	a	a	a	a	a	a	a	a	a	a	a	a
b	b	b	b	b	b	b	b	b	b	b	b	b	b
c	c	c	c	c	c	c	c	c	c	c	c	c	c
d	d	d	d	d	d	d	d	d	d	d	d	d	d
e	e	e	e	e	e	e	e	e	e	e	e	e	e

Bond 11+ Non-verbal Reasoning Test 3

Name

Section 1

Practice 1	Practice 2	1	2	3	4	5	6	7	8	9	10	11	12
a	a	a	a	a	a	a	a	a	a	a	a	a	a
b	b	b	b	b	b	b	b	b	b	b	b	b	b
c	c	c	c	c	c	c	c	c	c	c	c	c	c
d	d	d	d	d	d	d	d	d	d	d	d	d	d
e	e	e	e	e	e	e	e	e	e	e	e	e	e

Section 2

Practice 1	Practice 2	1	2	3	4	5	6	7	8	9	10	11	12
a	a	a	a	a	a	a	a	a	a	a	a	a	a
b	b	b	b	b	b	b	b	b	b	b	b	b	b
c	c	c	c	c	c	c	c	c	c	c	c	c	c
d	d	d	d	d	d	d	d	d	d	d	d	d	d
e	e	e	e	e	e	e	e	e	e	e	e	e	e

Section 3

Practice 1	Practice 2	1	2	3	4	5	6	7	8	9	10	11	12
a	a	a	a	a	a	a	a	a	a	a	a	a	a
b	b	b	b	b	b	b	b	b	b	b	b	b	b
c	c	c	c	c	c	c	c	c	c	c	c	c	c
d	d	d	d	d	d	d	d	d	d	d	d	d	d
e	e	e	e	e	e	e	e	e	e	e	e	e	e

Section 4

Practice 1	Practice 2	1	2	3	4	5	6	7	8	9	10	11	12
a	a	a	a	a	a	a	a	a	a	a	a	a	a
b	b	b	b	b	b	b	b	b	b	b	b	b	b
c	c	c	c	c	c	c	c	c	c	c	c	c	c
d	d	d	d	d	d	d	d	d	d	d	d	d	d
e	e	e	e	e	e	e	e	e	e	e	e	e	e

Section 5

Practice 1	Practice 2	1	2	3	4	5	6	7	8	9	10	11	12
a	a	a	a	a	a	a	a	a	a	a	a	a	a
b	b	b	b	b	b	b	b	b	b	b	b	b	b
c	c	c	c	c	c	c	c	c	c	c	c	c	c
d	d	d	d	d	d	d	d	d	d	d	d	d	d
e	e	e	e	e	e	e	e	e	e	e	e	e	e

Bond 11+ Non-verbal Reasoning Test 4

Name

Section 1

Practice 1	Practice 2	1	2	3	4	5	6
a b c d e	a b c d e	a b c d e	a b c d e	a b c d e	a b c d e	a b c d e	a b c d e

7	8	9	10	11	12
a b c d e	a b c d e	a b c d e	a b c d e	a b c d e	a b c d e

Section 2

Practice 1	Practice 2	1	2	3	4	5	6	7	8	9	10	11	12
a b c d e	a b c d e	a b c d e	a b c d e	a b c d e	a b c d e	a b c d e	a b c d e	a b c d e	a b c d e	a b c d e	a b c d e	a b c d e	a b c d e

Section 3

Practice 1	Practice 2	1	2	3	4	5	6	7	8	9	10	11	12
a b c d e	a b c d e	a b c d e	a b c d e	a b c d e	a b c d e	a b c d e	a b c d e	a b c d e	a b c d e	a b c d e	a b c d e	a b c d e	a b c d e

Section 4

Practice 1	Practice 2	1	2	3	4	5	6	7	8	9	10	11	12
a b c d e	a b c d e	a b c d e	a b c d e	a b c d e	a b c d e	a b c d e	a b c d e	a b c d e	a b c d e	a b c d e	a b c d e	a b c d e	a b c d e

Section 5

Practice 1	Practice 2	1	2	3	4	5	6	7	8	9	10	11	12
a b c d e	a b c d e	a b c d e	a b c d e	a b c d e	a b c d e	a b c d e	a b c d e	a b c d e	a b c d e	a b c d e	a b c d e	a b c d e	a b c d e

Bond 11+ Verbal Reasoning Test 1

Name

Example
e
f
n
k

1 g t k e

2 s l k o

3 t w p m

4 e a h o

5 f t r b

6 f y s w

7 o a e i

8 o s t e

Example
unkind
death
laughter
sad
friendly

9 alone, always, drink, quiet, quite

10 short, mile, high, low, desire

11 balm, tranquil, cream, storm, tide

12 bride, car, brush, vanish, stick

13 case, shorts, minimum, sudden, short

14 divide, fracture, whole, chorus, play

15 grass, garden, weed, unusual, ordinary

16 sum, hard, solution, difficulty, impossible

17
% ^ ! £
% ^ ~ £
£ ~ ^ £
% ^ ~ !

18
^ ! ~ #
! ^ % ~
! ~ ^ %
! ^ ~ %

19
% £ £ #
# £ £ %
! £ £ #
~ # # ^

20 SENSE, SINS, SELLS, SENILE

21 BEEN, LESS, LINE, LENS

22 ISLES, BIBLE, BELLS, BLESS

23
£ > < /
? / < >
? £ < !
? / > <

24
? $ / > ?
? $ / < <
> ? / $ $
< £ > ? ?

Example
Lions are cruel.
Lions are flesh.
Lions are not stone.
Lions are animals because they hunt.

25
Pictures consist of paint.
Monet liked poppies.
Monet was a painter.
Poppies need red paint.

26
Chairs can be made of wood.
Trees supply wood.
Wood is used for all furniture.
Trees are furniture because they are wood.

Example
LS GO GY | ON IO HO

27 DO CN CO | EQ DQ DP

28 XW UW MN | UV NM OM

29 FH HJ HI | NO MP NP

30 XI IX GW | VH WG WH

31 IJ IL JL | JM JJ IM

32 XX XR XU | VS VR VV

33 JKL jkl mno | ghi pqr PQR

34 Be aE Ae | Eg dH Dh

35 BY CY CZ | CX BA CY

Example
CAST
CASH
LAST
LUSH

36 WELD, WEND, WILD, WAND

37 CRIB, GRAB, CRAM, GLAD

38 WASH, PATH, PITS, WITH

39 SAIL, HALT, HOLT, SALE

40 JEEP, PEER, DEER, DEEP

41 STEP, PEST, MOPS, POTS

42 VENT, EVER, OMEN, OVEN

43 BOND, BIND, BEND, KINE

Example
we had
had bats
bats and
and balls

44
listen to
to her
her advice
advice carefully

45
my dentist
dentist opened
opened the
the surgery
surgery door

46
I wish
wish all
all my
my class
class could
could come
come to
to the
the party

CONTINUE

47

come to	to the
the back	back door
door of	of the
the new	new building

48

the squid	squid stretched
stretched a	a tentacle
tentacle over	over yellow
yellow weed	

49

take your	your litter
litter home	home never
never drop	drop it

50

the weather	weather forecast
forecast for	for this
this evening	evening is
is appalling	

51

the kite	kite string
string was	was caught
caught in	in the
the bush	

52

Paul	Judy
Peter	Beth
Toby	Suzy
Jon	Emily
Sue	Gary

53

Paul	Judy
Peter	Beth
Toby	Suzy
Jon	Emily
Sue	Gary

54

Paul	Judy
Peter	Beth
Toby	Suzy
Jon	Emily
Sue	Gary

Example

hand	light
green	house
for	sure

55

sun	shone
cloud	fall
rain	pour

56

moth	hop
ant	eater
frog	tick

57

act	role
play	cast
sausage	room

58

at	side
by	wide
in	last

59

hind	sight
right	deer
rain	fell

60

for	gear
four	place
fore	leg

61

up	left
under	right
stand	sit

62

to	age
by	way
in	held

Example

shunt	hip
hut	ship
shut	snip

63

duo	singe
due	sting
doe	stung

64

right	meter
fight	frame
tight	timer

65

read	rota
bead	riot
bred	brat

66

limb	stalk
slim	crack
clam	break

67

slay	rumble
spay	crumbs
play	crumple

68

lease	pills
pease	spill
place	still

69

rain	apple
tray	pleat
tail	treat

70

slit	pint
spit	sign
pile	spin

71

horse	burns
hoses	sunny
roses	basin

Example

tree	thin
short	white
colour	wide

72

colour	paint
crimson	cloud
danger	azure

73

impolite	unpleasant
rude	nasty
manners	sunny

74

hour	clock
tiny	time
second	huge

75

paint	artist
painter	page
brush	author

76

collar	saddle
paw	hoof
bark	stable

77

six	web
insect	eight
ladybird	spin

78

bedroom	football
sheet	chess
sleep	play

79

sty	milk
pork	moo
mud	cowshed

80

mountain	compost
ascend	age
descend	shrink

Bond 11+ Verbal Reasoning Test 2

Name

Example
we had
had bats
bats and
and balls

1
pigs eat
eat different
different sorts
sorts of
of scraps

2
please do
not leave
in such
a rush
do not
leave in
such a

3
Jack's solo
was in
the final
solo was
in the
final song

4
it would
be better
to go
another evening
would be
better to
go another

5
Sarah's car
would not
start this
car would
not start
this morning

6
climbing a
mountain is
challenge for
most people
a mountain
is a challenge
for most

7
biscuits often
contain high
levels of
often contain
high levels
of sugar

8
Amy immediately
posted her
cards as
she addressed
immediately posted
her cards
as she
addressed them

9
south
north
south east
south west

10
north west
south west
east
south

11
north west
north east
south
south west

12
1234
1243
1432
6234

13
6241
4621
6421
6124

14
STAR
YARD
DEAR
READ

15
DART
TRAY
STAR
ARTS

16
9345
5493
9348
5293

17
9345
5493
9348
5293

18
9345
5493
9348
5293

19
9345
5493
9348
5293

Example
stone
tyres
ration
nation
noisy

20
shard
dusty
thuds
rusty
hurry

21
staring
string
laser
grass
strain

22
nasty
stern
banter
rinse
tribe

23
house
honest
teeth
heels
those

24
swear
drawer
snared
swede
waned

25
fared
leader
flared
deaf
ladder

26
flower
fault
crow
frolic
crawl

27
fling
valour
gravel
grain
flour

28
drain
darts
dines
snare
nested

29
p
q
r
s
t

30
p
q
r
s
t

31
p
q
r
s
t

32
p
q
r
s
t

33
p
q
r
s
t

34
p
q
r
s
t

35
p
q
r
s
t

36
p
q
r
s
t

Example
price
hasten
strike
charge
money

37
weapon
spade
jewel
garden
heart

38
wedding
ring
line
valuable
rich

39
pile
fence
cheque
ditch
bank

40
stable
ride
house
reliable
sound

41
fraction
fork
cutlery
cut
food

42
fortify
key
bolt
escape
hide

43
suit
bond
chest
neck
tie

44
pursue
run
hound
jackal
hunt

45
pig
seed
farm
sow
hole

Example
e
f
n
k

46
f
t
r
b

47
s
w
k
f

48
l
r
e
w

49
b
a
g
t

Example
ps
ds
ch
ct

50
ch
th
br
st

51
la
er
sa
he

52
re
se
it
ts

53
ed
gr
be
le

Example
Lions are cruel.
Lions are flesh.
Lions are not stone.
Lions are animals because they hunt.

CONTINUE

54
My next door neighbour's house is made of brick.
My house is a cuboid.
My house is made of cuboid bricks.
All houses are brick.

55
Goldfish make good pets.
The seas are full of fish.
Goldfish breathe underwater.
Cod and mackerel live in the sea.

Example
CAST
CASH
LAST
LUSH

56 MESH, FIST, MAST, FAST

57 COAT, COST, COLT, COOL

58 TIER, TIRE, RITE, RATE

59 SEAT, TEAS, SEEM, TEAM

60 FOOT, POUR, POUT, FOUL

61 WINK, WINS, KIND, SINS

62 MADE, DAME, DAZE, DOME

63 LAIN, LAID, SANE, SAID

Example
race, shop, start | finish, begin, end

64 right, hand, finger | left, foot, correct

65 beloved, cheap, dear | expensive, love, antelope

66 tale, feeble, rat | small, mouse, fable

67 open, shut, window | closed, ajar, pane

68 weary, fresh, asleep | stale, tired, awake

69 kind, thoughtful, part | unkind, whole, sort

70 black, day, evening | white, night, light

71 pail, hind, fore | dark, three, buck

Example
11, 9, 10 | 15, 12, 16

72 3, 4, 5 | 6, 7, 8

73 24, 25, 26 | 32, 30, 33

74 58, 54, 56 | 49, 48, 50

75 20, 24, 22 | 28, 32, 30

76 17, 18, 45 | 20, 39, 42

77 1, 3, 2 | 16, 12, 20

78 5, 6, 7 | 10, 11, 12

79 9, 10, 36 | 17, 25, 30

80 6, 9, 4 | 8, 3, 2

Bond 11+ Verbal Reasoning Test 3

Name

1 q 5 m v, q m 5 v, q 2 m w, q v 5 m

2 2 w v 6, 2 m 5 v, 2 v m 6, 2 m v 6

3 FACT, CORE, CORN, CART

4 RIOT, RAIN, RACE, RATE

5 BASK, BAKE, TAKE, TASK

6 SAKE, SEEK, SOAK, SEED

7 7 x j 8, 7 x j 9, 7 j x 9, 7 j x 8

8 g 8 x 9 j, g 9 x 8 j, g 8 x j 9, g 8 x j 8

Example
Lions are cruel.
Lions are flesh.
Lions are not stone.
Lions are animals because they hunt.

9
Vegetables are green.
All green things are vegetables.
Vegetables are peas.
Peas are green vegetables.

10
Bees are sweet.
Everyone likes honey.
Bees can sting.
Bees make sweet honey.

11 Claire, Chris, Caroline | Nick, Sue, David

12 Claire, Chris, Caroline | Nick, Sue, David

13 Claire, Chris, Caroline | Nick, Sue, David

Example
we had
had bats
bats and
and balls

14
William please
please come
come at
at once

15
the sunset bathed the mountain in golden light | sunset bathed the mountain in golden

16
the river is flooding near my | river is flooding near my house

17
the pavement on our street is very uneven | pavement on our street is very

CONTINUE TO THE NEXT PAGE

18
we have
too much
homework tonight
have too
much homework

19
sailors told
of mermaids
combing their
golden tresses
told of
mermaids combing
their golden

20
the floorboards
are known
to be
structurally unsound
floorboards are
known to
be structurally

21
their apples
apples were
were apparently
apparently rotten

Example
tree, short, colour | thin, white, wide

22
air, fly, airport | water, periscope, metal

23
shirt, long, brief | belief, edible, amazing

24
cushion, bed, feathers | implement, spoon, hay

25
slow, quick, tight | sun, metal, dull

26
hard, easy, ardent | sacred, spooky, frightened

27
water, bank, boat | shady, tree, branch

28
bungalow, lumpy, house | warm, cold, icy

29
clean, see, lucid | clean, dirty, wash

30
eye, vision, cut | slice, spoon, utensil

Example
ps, ds, ch, ct

31
mb, sh, fl, el

32
ve, pe, me, re

33
an, rh, en, ar

34
ls, ra, hi, gu

35
se, ms, me, ha

36
in, re, de, ri

37
es, fi, so, ee

38
la, in, on, te

Example
LS, GO, GY | ON, IO, HO

39
VU, YV, NO | UV, OP, PO

40
OM, MN, OL | NM, LO, MO

41
AF, AH, AK | AG, AI, AL

42
CO, BO, DQ | CN, ER, EQ

43
ah, bh, cj | bi, ci, bj

44
WR, WX, WU | CD, DC, EF

45
Bh, Be, Ei | Bf, Ej, Ek

46
WX, XU, SQ | VW, TQ, ST

47
BX, VW, CX | GT, FT, HS

Example
broad, vague, long, narrow, motorway

48
downhill, crossing, even, uneven, upright

49
empty, drink, eaten, laden, replete

50
silent, motionless, active, photo, even

51
candle, wick, wane, ruby, dry

52
neighbour, opponent, mate, colleague, foe

53
flavour, tasteless, weak, robust, tasty

54
hour, second, tiny, vast, invisible

55
find, found, finding, finds, founded

Example
stone, tyres, ration, nation, noisy

56
shone, pole, photo, honest, spent

57
astute, suet, uses, sauce, states

58
fires, feast, spite, trees, rites

59
smith, chasm, match, charm, start

60
shade, rashes, dress, shares, drains

61
bleak, area, leer, bleed, rabble

62
state, tests, soap, taste, post

63
strove, sorry, overstay, very, store

64
singe, longing, ginger, lobes, gongs

Example
PETS, PENS, PEST | PENT, REST, PERT

65
CALF, COAL, PALM | MOLE, PILE, PALE

66
HARK, LAIR, LAKE | LAZE, HARE, MAZE

67
WART, WAIL, WAIT | JAIL, WARS, JUST

68
BITE, SIDE, SIRS | BILE, SILL, TILE

69
HAZE, DAZE, FAZE | FADE, MAZE, LAZE

70
FARE, FILE, FIRM | FILL, FURL, FAIL

71
KING, WING, SAND | SING, SANG, WIND

72
HUSH, MASH, FIST | MESH, MIST, MUSH

CONTINUE

73	74	75	76	77	78	79	80
11	12	21	21	19	20	22	25
13	10	18	19	17	21	21	20
14	11	20	20	16	22	20	22
9	9	17	22	18	19	23	24

Bond 11+ Verbal Reasoning Test 4

Name

Example	
dawn	late
early	stop
awake	sunrise

1	
open	closed
shut	ajar
near	unfenced

2	
skin	burden
hide	look
bear	seek

3	
tight	fast
noose	loose
slack	hang

4	
boiling	cooler
warm	sweat
hot	freezing

5	
begun	ended
begin	ending
finished	ends

6	
under	out
on	below
in	through

7	
moon	star
light	sky
night	dark

8	
fine	dress
fancy	dirty
ill	thick

9	10	11	12	13	14	15	16
A	A	A	A	A	A	A	A
B	B	B	B	B	B	B	B
C	C	C	C	C	C	C	C
D	D	D	D	D	D	D	D
E	E	E	E	E	E	E	E

Example	
hand	light
green	house
for	sure

17	
tree	picker
wood	pecker
branch	packer

18	
star	trek
house	super
home	light

19	
board	cup
coffee	room
runner	been

20	
flow	slow
break	fast
time	minute

21	
short	about
fall	circle
round	climb

22	
through	sign
in	full
though	out

23	
some	even
who	ever
odd	out

24	
through	all
by	hold
out	come

Example	
shunt	hip
hut	ship
shut	snip

25	
arrow	thank
hurry	trunk
heron	think

26	
rank	paths
rink	patch
cram	parch

27	
light	flame
fight	cream
tight	camel

28	
ream	creed
reach	bread
cram	breed

29	
rain	break
clan	creek
cane	beach

CONTINUE TO THE NEXT PAGE

30
toes, hose, hoes | hens, then, hone

31
trough, tough, though | frog, flog, thug

32
bat, oat, boa | music, bemuse, mouse

33
ray, star, arts | hovers, hooves, them

34
one, two, three, four | five, six, seven, eight

35
1, 2, 3, 4 | 5, 6, 7, 8

36
1, 2, 3, 4 | 5, 6, 7, 8

Example
PETS, PENS, PEST | PENT, REST, PERT

37
TALE, MALT, SALT | HILT, SILT, TILT

38
HOPE, HARD, HARE | HERE, HIRE, HEAR

39
SUEZ, QUIT, QUIN | SUIT, SEAT, DUET

40
STEM, SOUP, STEP | SEEM, SEEP, SEAM

41
PINT, WINK, WINE | WIND, WAIL, WANT

42
WARS, SCAR, CURS | PART, CART, WART

43
POST, MAST, PAST | MARK, PARK, PORT

44
FARM, FILE, FEEL | POLE, PILE, PALE

Example
price, hasten, strike, charge, money

45
scene, part, leave, school, sum

46
shell, tide, recognise, see, wave

47
price, dear, sweet, cheap, kind

48
possess, ore, mine, belong, pit

49
stick, leaf, tree, tack, mend

50
second, examine, tell, follow, watch

51
bridle, groom, jump, hat, bell

52
dustbin, lorry, tip, litter, table

53
may, gun, spring, boot, march

Example
11, 9, 10 | 15, 12, 16

54
20, 18, 22 | 23, 24, 21

55
55, 50, 48 | 35, 30, 28

56
25, 30, 20 | 40, 50, 60

57
35, 20, 33 | 15, 18, 24

58
51, 13, 15 | 61, 71, 19

59
3, 6, 8 | 48, 72, 36

60
32, 30, 3 | 6, 33, 20

61
8, 16, 24 | 28, 30, 32

62
4, 6, 16 | 12, 10, 8

Example
we had, had bats, bats and, and balls

63
dates can, be found, on palm | can be, found on, palm trees

64
please attach, your pencils, to your | attach your, pencils to, your clipboards

65
the small, boy lost, his mother, in the | small boy, lost his, mother in, the crowd

66
Tom's spectacular, save ensured, victory for, the home | spectacular save, ensured victory, for the, home side

67
waves tumbled, and crashed, on the | tumbled and, crashed on, the shingle

68
the cheetah, can reach, incredible speeds, over short | cheetah can, reach incredible, speeds over, short distances

69
an old, man fell, on the, ice and, broke his | old man, fell on, the ice, and broke, his hip

70
Amy wanted, to sit, on the, row in, front of | wanted to, sit on, the row, in front, of Neil

71
g s p l, g p s l, g s l p, p g s l

72
t q q p o, t t p q o, t q p p o, t q p o o

73
KNITS, KNOWN, KNIFE, KNEEL

74
SAWING, SALADS, SAUNAS, SAUCER

75
TONG, TOMB, TOUR, TOME

76
GRAVEL, GORGON, GROUND, GROUPS

77
c y p r f, c p y r f, c y p f r, b z p r f

78
j u m c q r, j m u c r q, j u m c r q, j m u c q r

Example
Lions are cruel.
Lions are flesh.
Lions are not stone.
Lions are animals because they hunt.

79
Shoes are worn with socks.
All shoes are made from leather.
Leather shoes are waterproof.
Leather is the best material for shoes.

80
All words are written.
Sentences are made of words.
Letters are always written with a pen.
Words can be written.